Quotable Cats

Milly Brown

summersdale

QUOTABLE CATS

Summersdale Publishers Ltd
46 West Street
Chichester
West Sussex
PO19 1RP
UK

www.summersdale.com

Printed and bound in China

ISBN: 978-1-84953-617-2

Substantial discounts on bulk quantities of Summersdale books are available to corporations, professional associations and other organisations. For details contact Nicky Douglas by telephone: +44 (0) 1243 756902, fax: +44 (0) 1243 786300 or email: nicky@summersdale.com.

Introduction

Every cat owner knows the joys of being woken by a gentle (or not so gentle) paw-swipe in the face, finding hairs all over your best jumper and facing the dilemma of how to remove a sleeping cat from your laptop without initiating a major feline sulk. This wonderful collection of beautiful photographs and uplifting quotations celebrates all that's best about our furry friends.

Cats are living adornments.

Edwin Lent

THERE ARE FEW THINGS IN LIFE MORE HEARTWARMING THAN TO BE WELCOMED BY A CAT.

Tay Hohoff

Cats can work out mathematically the exact place to sit that will cause most inconvenience.

Pam Brown

THERE ARE TWO MEANS OF REFUGE FROM THE MISERIES OF LIFE: MUSIC AND CATS.

Albert Schweitzer

There is, incidentally, no way of talking about cats that enables one to come off as a sane person.

Dan Greenberg

THE IDEAL OF CALM EXISTS IN A SITTING CAT.

Jules Renard

The cat could very
well be man's best
friend but would never
stoop to admitting it.

Doug Larson

Dogs come when they're called; cats take a message and get back to you later.

Mary Bly

Prose books are the show dogs I breed and sell to support my cat.

Robert Graves

AFTER SCOLDING
ONE'S CAT ONE
LOOKS INTO ITS FACE
AND IS SEIZED BY
THE UGLY SUSPICION
THAT IT UNDERSTOOD
EVERY WORD.

Charlotte Gray

Lettin' the cat out of the bag is a whole lot easier 'n puttin' it back in.

Will Rogers

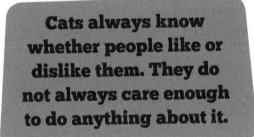

Cats always know whether people like or dislike them. They do not always care enough to do anything about it.

Winifred Carrière

It was difficult to feel
vexed by a creature
that burst into a
chorus of purring.

Philip Brown

DON'T LET ANYONE
TELL YOU LOVING A
CAT IS SILLY. LOVE,
IN ANY FORM, IS A
PRECIOUS COMMODITY.

Barbara L. Diamond

Some people have cats and go on to lead normal lives.

Anonymous

IF ONLY CATS GREW INTO KITTENS.

Robert A. M. Stern

The mathematical probability of a common cat doing exactly as it pleases is the one scientific absolute in the world.

Lynn M. Osband

Even overweight cats instinctively know the cardinal rule: when fat, arrange yourself in slim poses.

John Weitz

THERE IS NO SNOOZE BUTTON ON A CAT WHO WANTS BREAKFAST.

Anonymous

THE DIFFERENCE BETWEEN FRIENDS AND PETS IS THAT FRIENDS WE ALLOW INTO OUR COMPANY, PETS WE ALLOW INTO OUR SOLITUDE.

Robert Brault

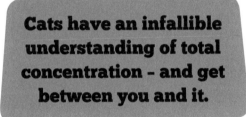

Cats have an infallible understanding of total concentration – and get between you and it.

Arthur Bridges

ONLY CAT LOVERS
KNOW THE LUXURY OF
FUR-COATED, MUSICAL
HOT-WATER BOTTLES
THAT DON'T GO COLD.

Suzanne Millen

Cats pride themselves on their ability to do nothing.

John R. F. Breen

An ordinary kitten will
ask more questions than
any five-year-old.

Carl Van Vechten

DOGS HAVE OWNERS, CATS HAVE STAFF.

Anonymous

Your cat will
never threaten your
popularity by barking
at three in the morning.

Helen Powers

Laziness is nothing more
than the habit of resting
before you get tired.

Jules Renard

THE DOG MAY BE WONDERFUL PROSE, BUT ONLY THE CAT IS POETRY.

French proverb

Meow is like aloha – it can mean anything.

Hank Ketchum

No amount of masking tape can ever totally remove [a cat's] fur from your couch.

Leo Dworken

TO A CAT, 'NO!' MEANS 'NOT WHILE I'M LOOKING.'

Anonymous

Two cats can live as cheaply as one, and their owner has twice as much fun.

Lloyd Alexander

The cat that is kissing you lovingly has just devoured a rabbit and has left the entrails under the bed.

Anonymous

PEOPLE MEETING
FOR THE FIRST TIME
SUDDENLY RELAX
IF THEY FIND THEY
BOTH HAVE CATS.
AND PLUNGE INTO
ANECDOTE.

Charlotte Gray

I had been told that the training procedure with cats was difficult...
Mine had me trained in two days.

Bill Dana

SOME PEOPLE ARE
BORN INTO CAT-
LOVING FAMILIES,
SOME ACHIEVE CATS
AND SOME HAVE CATS
THRUST UPON THEM.

William H. A. Carr

All of the animals except
for man know that the
principal business of life
is to enjoy it.

Samuel Butler

HIS FRIENDSHIP
IS NOT EASILY
WON BUT IT
IS SOMETHING
WORTH HAVING.

M. K. Joseph

Like children, cats
exist on a separate and
probably higher plane
than we do.

Peter Gethers

Even if you have just destroyed a Ming vase, purr. Usually all will be forgiven.

Lenny Rubenstein

I have studied many philosophers and many cats. The wisdom of cats is infinitely superior.

Hippolyte Taine

A BLACK CAT CROSSING
YOUR PATH SIGNIFIES
THAT THE ANIMAL IS
GOING SOMEWHERE.

Groucho Marx

Most cats, when they are out want to be in, and vice versa, and often simultaneously.

Louis J. Camuti

Cats' hearing apparatus is built to allow the human voice to easily go in one ear and out the other.

Stephen Baker

I DON'T KNOW HE'S THERE UNTIL I YAWN AND MY MOUTH CLOSES ON A WHISKER.

Astrid Alauda on sleeping with her cat

No matter how much cats
fight, there always seem
to be plenty of kittens.

Abraham Lincoln

A CREATURE THAT NEVER CRIES OVER SPILT MILK: A CAT.

Evan Esar

LIKE A GRACEFUL
VASE, A CAT, EVEN
WHEN MOTIONLESS,
SEEMS TO FLOW.

George F. Will

Cats seem to go on the principle that it never does any harm to ask for what you want.

Joseph Wood Krutch

It's the fact that they have to spend a good part of the day putting their hair back in place.

Debbie Peterson on why cats dislike baths

A CAT HAS NINE LIVES. FOR THREE HE PLAYS, FOR THREE HE STRAYS AND FOR THE LAST THREE HE STAYS.

English proverb

There is no such thing as 'just a cat'.

Robert A. Heinlein

BY THE TIME MY
KEY HITS THE LOCK
I HEAR THE SOFT
PRESS OF PAWS ON
THE OTHER SIDE OF
THE DOOR.

Gwen Cooper

Cat: a pygmy lion who loves mice, hates dogs and patronises human beings.

Oliver Herford

PEOPLE THAT
DON'T LIKE CATS
HAVEN'T MET THE
RIGHT ONE YET.

Deborah A. Edwards

What happens if you
strap buttered toast
to the back of a cat?

Steven Wright

MOST BEDS SLEEP
UP TO SIX CATS.
TEN CATS WITHOUT
THE OWNER.

Stephen Baker

Who among us hasn't envied a cat's ability to ignore the cares of daily life and to relax completely?

Karen Brademeyer

In ancient times cats were worshipped as gods; they have not forgotten this.

Terry Pratchett

Cats are kindly masters, just so long as you remember your place.

Paul Gray

Dogs eat. Cats dine.

Ann Taylor

IF THERE WERE TO
BE A UNIVERSAL
SOUND DEPICTING
PEACE, I WOULD
SURELY VOTE FOR
THE PURR.

Barbara L. Diamond

If you're interested in finding out more about our books, find us on Facebook at **Summersdale Publishers** and follow us on Twitter at **@Summersdale**.

www.summersdale.com